Copyright © 2025 Catch a Leaf Publishing

All rights reserved. This book or any portion thereof may not be reproduced or used in any manner whatsoever without the express written permission of the publisher, except in the case of brief quotations embodied in a review and certain other non-commercial uses permitted by copyright law.

ISBN Paperback: 978-1-0684694-1-1
ISBN Hardback: 978-10686122-9-9

Text and Illustrations by Siski Kalla
Design Audrey Sauble
Published by Catch a Leaf Publishing

Also available in the series:
Let's Explore Snails, Let's Explore Ducks

JNF037020 JUVENILE NONFICTION / Science & Nature / Environmental Conservation & Protection
NAT045000 NATURE / Ecosystems & Habitats / General
JNF003170 JUVENILE NONFICTION / Animals / Pets
JNF051000 JUVENILE NONFICTION / Science & Nature / General

First Edition, 2025

To all the children growing up in towns and cities who love nature.

To all the children who'll move a snail off the path, scoop a ladybird out of water, and gently capture a moth to release it outside.

To all the children who care about wildlife – you are amazing!

Let's explore moths!

Can you answer this question for me?

What makes a moth a moth?

A moth flies! It has wings.

But so do butterflies*, birds, and even bats! So what other thing makes a moth a moth?

*Although both moths and butterflies have wings, moths rest with their wings open so you can see the upper sides. Butterflies usually rest with their wings together or closed, so you see only the undersides.

A moth has six legs!

Birds and bats don't have six legs. This means that moths are insects, like butterflies, flies, bees, wasps, and this crane fly (aka daddy long legs) to the right.

I've always fancied myself as a pigeon, actually.

You may have wings, but you've only got two legs. So you're not a moth or an insect!

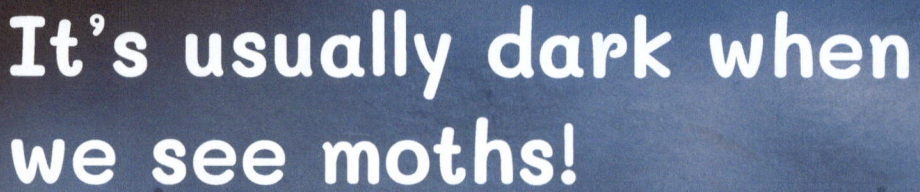

It's usually dark when we see moths!

Moths seem to love light! They're always flying towards lights in our homes and on the streets!

Many moths only fly at night, but some fly in the day!

Moths are often grey, white, or brown so they're not easily seen. But some are brightly coloured just like a butterfly! If you look closely, you'll see they are all beautiful!

Snails are also beautiful!

So if it's an insect, has wings, flies at night or day, can be colourful, **what makes a moth a moth and not a butterfly?**

A moth metamorphoses (that means it changes its form) from a caterpillar to a winged adult in a different way to a butterfly.

Keep it down! I'm trying to transform in here!

A moth has a life cycle similar to that of a butterfly but there is an important difference.

A female moth mates with a male moth, then she lays eggs.

Tip: look for Jersey Tiger eggs on nettles and brambles

After a time, the eggs hatch into caterpillars.

The caterpillar eats, growing bigger, until it pupates (change into a new form). This is where butterflies are different – they make a chrysalis while a moth usually makes a cocoon.

Once it has changed form, safe in its cocoon, it's ready to emerge then fly!

Pupa

Cocoon (pupa is inside)

A chrysalis is smooth and made of a kind of hardened skin of the butterfly, while a cocoon has the moth pupa inside (like a sleeping bag!), and this will be discarded when the moth emerges. You might be lucky and find an empty pupa!

What else makes a moth a moth and not a butterfly?

Moths have a pair of antennae, like butterflies. But moths' antennae are different.

Most butterflies rest with their wings closed, like this, so you don't see the colourful pattern. Moths usually rest with their wings open.

Hey there, grasshopper, what's hoppening?!

Nothing much. Just crickets around here!

Use a magnifying glass to look at a moth up close or take a digital photo and zoom in.

You'll see that butterflies have very thin 'clubbed' antennae – they have very thin antennae with a thicker part at the ends.

Moths often have feathery antennae, and they are more horizontal, too (grow out to the sides rather than upwards). This is to help the males 'smell' if there's a female moth nearby to mate with.

Moths' antennae are usually angled sideways from the head, while a butterfly's protrude upwards.

I'd like to be able to smell with antennae too!

The easiest way to know it's a moth and not a butterfly? Look for them at nighttime!

Although we've seen that there are some moths that fly in the day, there are no butterflies that fly at night. So if it's nighttime you can be sure it's a moth.

Why do moths fly towards light?

Lepidopterists (scientists who study butterflies/moths) aren't sure! Some think it's because they use moonlight to navigate, others think it's to escape danger, and one study suggested that moths become 'trapped' in the glow of light. What do you think?

Moths are safer at night

Lots of moth predators (animals that eat moths) aren't around at night, so that helps keep them safe!

Magpie

Bluetit

Robin

Moth caterpillar

Some animals eat moths only during their caterpillar stage, others eat them only during their adult/flying stage. And some animals, especially birds, will eat them both!

Buff–tip moth, *Phalera bucephala*

In what other ways can moths stay safe from predators?

How do I stay safe? By looking just like a piece of bark or a twig. I tuck my wings in and even my antennae. If you spot me in the wild you must be a great observologist!

"You can see me now, but I'm hard to spot on tree bark!"

Many moths use their wing colouring and pattern to hide from predators.

Some moths, though, have colours or patterns that scare off predators. When an oak eggar (right) opens its wings fully it reveals 'eye shapes' on its wings that startle predators so they leave it alone.

"Do you think my eye spots make me look startling?"

Some moths even make sounds to scare predators away! Garden tiger moths (right), for example, will make a clicking sound to try and put even bats off their trail.

What do moths eat?

Most moths use their proboscis to feed on nectar from flowers, juices from damaged fruit, or tree sap. A proboscis is like a long curled up drinking straw.

Nectar, sweet sticky nectar... I'm going to use my long curly tongue to eat it!

But remember that moths were also caterpillars at one stage in their life cycle! So while moths may feed on nectar or fruits, caterpillars might eat leaves, fruit, bark or even your clothes! This is often what gets moths 'in trouble' with humans.

Some moths lay their eggs inside fruit or crop foods. This can make it difficult for farmers to sell their products, because no one wants an apple with a 'worm' inside!

"Whoopsies. I was hungry!"

The horse-chestnut leaf miner moth's larvae eat the leaves of the conker tree. You might notice shrivelled and half-eaten leaves.

Some moths eat the same food as us! If pantry moths (*Plodia interpunctella*) lay eggs in nuts or rice they might hatch before you eat them, then fly out when you open the packaging!

To protect fruit trees, plants, food or clothes, you can use moth traps instead of insecticides (which kill other insects too). These prevent breeding. They use a pheremone (a scent) that attracts males to the trap.

Moths can cause problems!

You may have heard of some moths eating clothes! It's true, except it's not the flying adult moths that do the munching, it's the little larvae that hatch from the eggs they've laid on your clothes.

My favourite top! I'll have to mend it with some pretty embroidery.

Clothes-eating moths will feast on natural textiles such as wool, fur and feathers but not on artificial (man-made) fibres. To protect your clothes, use cedar blocks which release a smell the moths don't like. Or you can seal your clothing in air-tight containers.

Moth Menu
Cotton T-shirt
Wool jumper
Silk scarf

Today's Special: Cashmere!

Ooh, cashmere! My babies will love it!

Also, be aware that moths prefer clothes that aren't completely clean! So even if you've only worn your Christmas jumper once, wash it before you store it away for another year!

I found a tiny bit of gravy! Nothing like a bit of old food on wool for a first meal. Delicious!

Are moths in trouble? Yes, they are.

All insects are in danger and moths are especially at risk because some species rely on specific flowers or plants that humans consider weeds.

Habitat loss The more we build in green areas, the less space moths have to live.

Urban lighting is also a problem. If moths are confused by artificial light, they spend less time feeding or breeding.

Monocultures (When only one type of plant is grown over large areas.) This means fewer wild plants and no variety of flowers for moths to feed from.

Moths are important!

Moths are pollinators! Just like butterflies and bees, moths help fertilise plants, flowers and trees by moving pollen from one plant to another as they feed on the nectar.

Moths are also indicator species which means they let us know if an area is doing well or not, in terms of plants and wildlife.

Can you help moths? Yes, you can!

At school
Talk to your teacher about adding a variety of plants, grasses and flowers in the outside area.

Help Save Moths
✗ No pesticides
✗ No herbicides
✗ Lights off
✓ Plants
✓ Speak up!

At home

Plant flowers in your garden or in pots on your balcony. Not just any flowers, though, choose ones that smell stronger in the evening (ideal for most moths). Jasmine, evening primrose, and honeysuckle are some you could try.

Don't kill the weeds! (This is what herbicide is – a weed killer.) Moths (and butterflies) love nettles, dandelions, clover, too.

Leave some areas wild, and don't be too tidy! Leave some leaf piles, fallen twigs or branches, so that any caterpillars or pupae can survive on them until spring.

Pesticides that kill insects will also kill moths, so don't use those.

Use your voice!

Gather signatures from other children in your school or street to ask the council to plant and protect more native trees and plants. Ask your parents or a teacher to help.

Report moths you've seen to citizen science projects via Earthwatch, or using apps such as iRecord.co.uk.

"I'm using an old ice cream tub. It's wide so I won't hurt the moth."

Sometimes a moth accidentally flies inside – into your house, shed, or even a classroom.

It's important to try and avoid damaging the moth's fragile wings. Use a large container (round is best) to place over the moth.

Then use a piece of sturdy paper or card to slide under.

Open the window or take it outside and allow the moth to fly out.

"I'm freeee!"

Have a Moth Treasure Hunt to see how many moths you can find

On a dry evening, hang an old white sheet in the garden and shine a torch onto it. Watch as moths land and make a note of what they look like.

Light! I'm mesmerised!

Moths you might see in your street, local park or back garden

Tips to find moths: look for brown, grey patterned moths or caterpillars on branches or tree trunks; look for green caterpillars on green leaves/plants. Remember that some moths are diurnal (awake mostly during the day), while others are nocturnal, and some can be spotted during night or day.

Elephant hawkmoth, *Deilephila elpenor*

I have 'eyes' on my face that aren't real eyes. They're just a pattern! Scary, eh?!

Hawkmoth caterpillars are green when they first emerge. They have a 'hook' at one end which makes them easy to identify.

Oh wow, I just LOVE your hair!

Sycamore moth, *Acronicta aceris*

Moths are everywhere! And they travel too!

Moths can be found in cities, woodland, rainforests, coastlines, deserts, and even in icy cold regions like the Arctic!

Worldwide there are thought to be more than 160,000 species of moth. And you can find lots of species of moths just by looking in one small urban garden!

I travel, too. Today I'm going to France on a cheese-tasting tour, via Rat-Rail. How are you travelling?

I fly via wing power!

In winter (Northern Hemisphere), moths fly from Europe to Africa, and in summer, they'll head northwards.

Death's head hawk moth

Some moths migrate, just like some birds, swallows, for example – and people, too!

The Silver Y migrates to northerly parts of Europe for summer, and to southerly parts of Europe and Northern Africa, for winter.

Silver Y

Certain species fly all the way from Europe or even North Africa to be in the UK, to avoid dry, hot summers farther south. They'll also migrate south, to avoid the long cold winters!

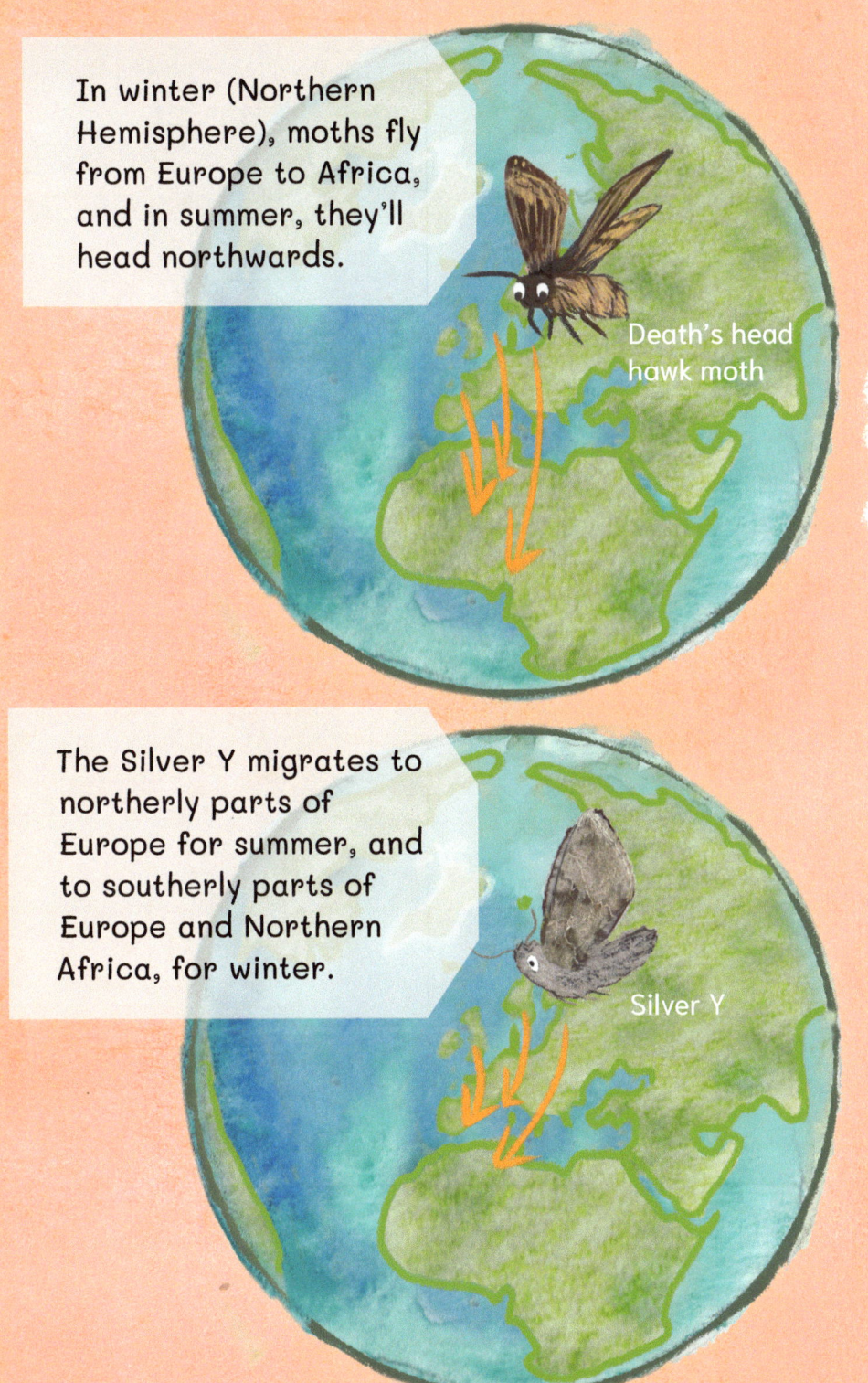

Make a Moth Mobile!

Art recipe ingredients

kitchen paper towel (toilet paper also works but only if it's strong/thick)

glue

water-based paints or felt tip markers

some twine or string/thread

scissors

stick/coat hanger

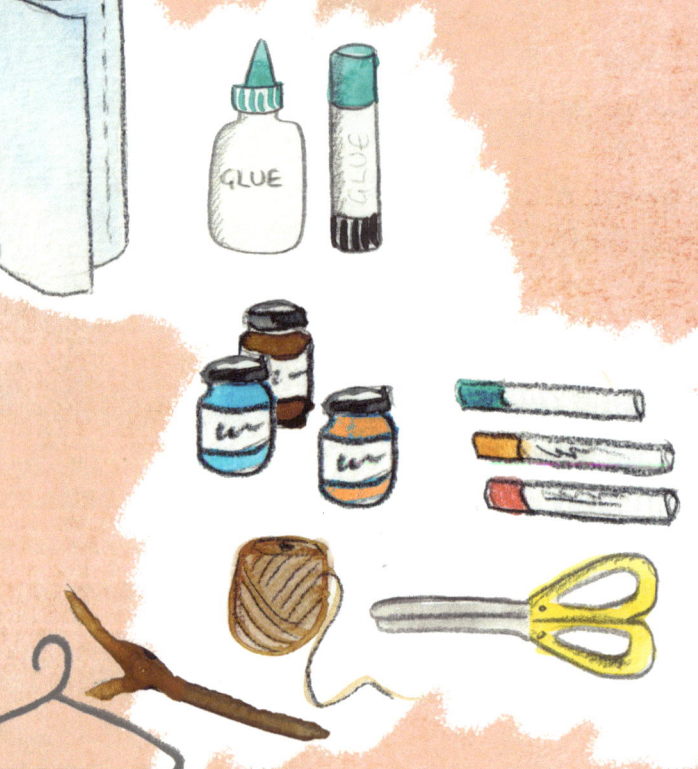

What to do

1) Fold a piece of square kitchen towel like a concertina.

2) Dot your felt-tip markers, Sharpies, watercolour paint on to the kitchen paper. It will spread quickly! So you don't need a lot.

3) Once coloured and dried, fold it in half towards the centre. Secure it with twine or string.

4) Glue a body to the moth if you like. I used small twigs and some catkins from a birch tree. See what you can find outside!

5) Now tie your moths with string to a stick or an unused coat hanger. Watch as your moths flutter in the breeze!

earthwatch EUROPE

Earthwatch Europe

Every purchase of this book is a positive change for our planet. For every sale of this book 50p goes to support Earthwatch Europe, an environmental charity with science at its heart.

Earthwatch works to create a world where we live in balance with nature by helping people to protect the nature around them. Earthwatch builds meaningful nature connections and gives people the tools they need to fight for our planet. Working alongside communities and organisations, Earthwatch builds an understanding and a love of nature, and helps everyone to protect the natural world. Guided by science and powered by people, Earthwatch creates change through connection.

Find out more at Earthwatch.org.uk

Some other organisations to check out:

UK Moths

If you're struggling to ID a moth, this is a great place to look. You can also help by getting involved in the National Moth Recording Scheme (NMRS) . Visit https://ukmoths.org.uk

Butterfly Conservation

This wildlife organisation also covers moths and other insects, not just butterflies! They have special reserves, collect data, and there are lots of opportunities for you to get involved, too. Visit https://butterfly-conservation.org

Can you find all of these hiding in the book?

I'm Siski, the author and illustrator of this book – and also *Let's Explore Ducks*, and *Let's Explore Snails* (pictured right). I look so happy in the photo because *Let's Explore Snails* won an award from the Society of Children's Book Writers and Illustrators! That made me very happy, as you can see.

I used to think moths were the 'boring' versions of butterflies. But that's because I didn't know moths! I also admit that when I first took a macro (extreme close-up) photo of a December moth I thought, 'Awww, it looks so fluffy and cuddly!' (I didn't try to cuddle it, I know that would hurt a moth.) Moths are amazing! I hope you love them as much as I do.

Illustration note: You might notice that I've given the moths in this book eyes a bit like ours. In reality, moths have compound eyes (as do butterflies). This means their eyes are made up of thousands of little 'eyes' or lenses, which helps them see in the dark, too!

www.ingramcontent.com/pod-product-compliance
Lightning Source LLC
Chambersburg PA
CBHW041535040426
42446CB00002B/104